FIRST SCIENCE

Sound

by Kay Manolis

Consultant:
Duane Quam, M.S. Physics
Chair, Minnesota State
Academic Science Standards
Writing Committee

BLASTOFF! 4 READERS

BELLWETHER MEDIA · MINNEAPOLIS, MN

Note to Librarians, Teachers, and Parents:

Blastoff! Readers are carefully developed by literacy experts and combine standards-based content with developmentally-appropriate text.

Level 1 provides the most support through repetition of high-frequency words, light text, predictable sentence patterns, and strong visual support.

Level 2 offers early readers a bit more challenge through varied simple sentences, increased text load, and less repetition of high frequency words.

Level 3 advances early-fluent readers toward fluency through increased text and concept load, less reliance on visuals, longer sentences, and more literary language.

Level 4 builds reading stamina by providing more text per page, increased use of punctuation, greater variation in sentence patterns, and increasingly challenging vocabulary.

Level 5 encourages children to move from "learning to read" to "reading to learn" by providing even more text, varied writing styles, and less familiar topics.

Whichever book is right for your reader, Blastoff! Readers are the perfect books to build confidence and encourage a love of reading that will last a lifetime!

This edition first published in 2008 by Bellwether Media.

No part of this publication may be reproduced in whole or in part without written permission of the publisher. For information regarding permission, write to Bellwether Media Inc., Attention: Permissions Department, Post Office Box 1C, Minnetonka, MN 55345-9998.

Library of Congress Cataloging-in-Publication Data
Manolis, Kay.
  Sound / by Kay Manolis.
    p. cm. – (Blastoff! readers. First science)
Summary: "First Science explains introductory physical science concepts about sound through real-world observation and simple scientific diagrams. Intended for students in grades three through six"—Provided by publisher.
  Includes bibliographical references and index.
  ISBN-13: 978-1-60014-099-0 (hardcover : alk. paper)
  ISBN-10: 1-60014-099-8 (hardcover : alk. paper)
1. Sound–Juvenile literature. 2. Sound–Measurement–Juvenile literature. I. Title.

  QC225.5.M36 2008
  534–dc22   2007021059

Contents

What Is Sound?

Stop and listen! What do you hear? Do you hear a dog barking? Is a plane flying overhead? Is someone playing music?

Sounds are all around you. They help you learn about the world.

fun fact

Crickets have ears on their legs.

Sounds are made by small movements called **vibrations**. When you hit a drum, you make its surface vibrate. This makes the air next to the drum vibrate. You can't see the vibrations, but they move away from the drum in all directions. Vibrations that move through the air are called **sound waves**.

Sound waves enter your ears. They make small bones and other parts inside your ear vibrate. These vibrations inside your ear send messages to your brain. You hear sounds when the messages reach your brain.

All sounds are different, but they all start with vibrations. Strumming guitar strings makes the strings vibrate. Blowing into a recorder makes the air vibrate inside the recorder.

Some vibrations move faster than others.
Faster vibrations have a higher **pitch**.
A recorder makes a high-pitched sound.

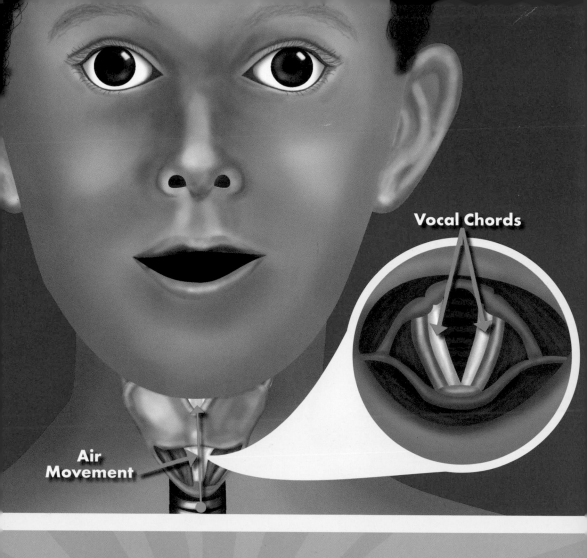

Vocal Chords

Air Movement

The sounds you make start with vibrations too! You have a **voice box** inside your neck that holds **vocal cords**. When you talk or sing, you force air from your lungs through your voice box. The forced air makes your vocal cords vibrate.

Touch the front of your neck as you talk or sing. Do you feel the vibrations in your vocal cords?

! fun fact

Sound travels slower than light. In a thunderstorm, you see lightning before you hear thunder even though they happen at the same time.

Sounds can be quiet or loud. When you whisper, you gently push a small amount of air over your vocal cords. The vibrations make a quiet sound.

When you shout, you push a lot of
air very hard over your vocal cords.
This makes bigger vibrations. Bigger
vibrations make a louder sound.

Measuring Sound

The volume of sounds can be measured in **decibels**. Rustling leaves measure around 10 decibels. Normal talking measures around 35 decibels.

A chainsaw at work measures around 110 decibels. A sound that loud can damage your ears. Workers wear earplugs to protect their ears from loud sounds.

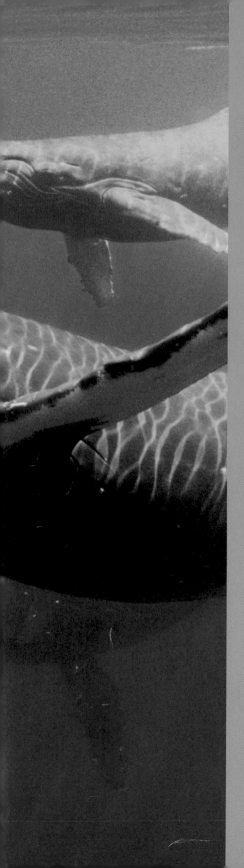

Sound waves travel through water in the same way they travel through air. In fact, they travel much faster through water than they do through air. Whales make sounds underwater. Other whales hear the sounds. This helps whales find each other.

fun fact

A humpback whale's sounds can be heard by other humpbacks up to 100 miles (161 kilometers) away.

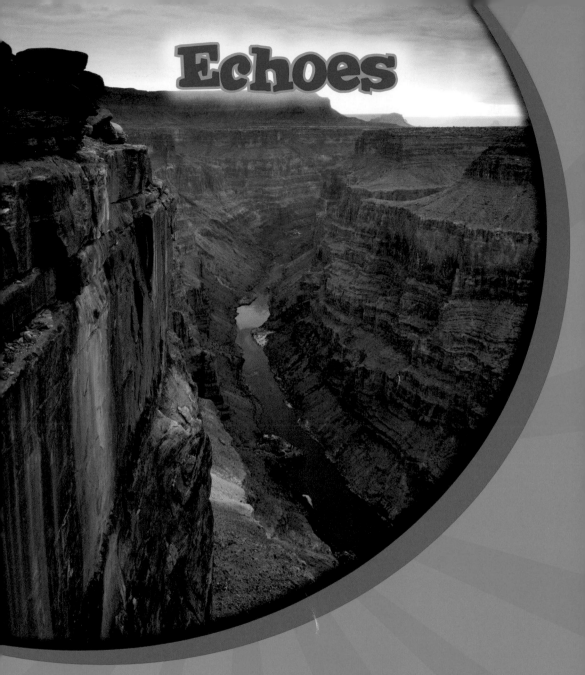

Echoes

Have you ever heard an **echo**? An echo is a sound wave that bounces off of a big surface such as a rock wall. The sound wave comes back to you and you hear the sound again.

Some animals use echoes to find their way around. Bats make sounds as they fly. They listen for their sounds to bounce off of objects around them. Echoes tell them the location of objects.

Sounds tell you many things. A siren on an ambulance tells people there is an emergency. Drivers hear the siren and move their cars out of the way so the ambulance can bring help quickly.

Thank goodness for sounds! Sounds help you in many ways. Sounds can keep you safe. Sounds also make life interesting and more fun.

21

Glossary

decibels—a unit for measuring the volume of sounds

echo—a sound heard again because it has bounced off of something

pitch—the tone of a sound; low sounds have a low pitch and high sounds have a high pitch.

sound wave—a series of vibrations in a gas, liquid, or solid; the movement can enter the ear and be heard as sound.

vibration—a fast movement back and forth

vocal cords—body parts in the neck that vibrate and make sound

voice box—the part of the body that holds the vocal cords

To Learn More

AT THE LIBRARY
Meachen Rau, Dana. *So Many Sounds*. New York: Children's Press, 2000.

Pfeffer, Wendy. *Sounds All Around*. New York: HarperCollins, 1999.

Rosinsky, Natalie. *Sound: Loud, Soft, High, and Low*. Minneapolis, Minn.: Picture Window Books, 2002.

ON THE WEB
Learning more about sound is as easy as 1, 2, 3.

1. Go to www.factsurfer.com

2. Enter "sound" into search box.

3. Click the "Surf" button and you will see a list of related web sites.

With factsurfer.com, finding more information is just a click away.

Index

The images in this book are reproduced through the courtesy of: Juan Martinez, front cover; David Woolley, pp. 4-5; Mel Yates/Getty Images, pp. 6-7; Nicolas Manu, p. 8; David Deas, p. 9; Steve Skjold/ Alamy, p. 10; WizData, Inc, pp. 11-12; Cliff Parnell, p. 13; VEER Steven Puetzer/Getty Images, p. 14; Bateleur, p. 15; Masa Ushioda/imagequestmarine, pp. 16-17; Eric Foltz, p. 18; Philip Date, p. 19; Dennis MacDonald, pp. 20-21.